THE BEATLES • WINGS • BEATLEMANIA • THE RUTLES • A HARD DAY'S NIGHT • HELP! • YELLOW SUBMARINE • LET IT BE • SERGEANT PEPPER'S LONELY HEARTS CLUB BAND

Here, in 100 fact-filled quizzes, is everything the most tried-and-true Beatles fan could possibly know about John, Paul, George, and Ringo—their Liverpool origins to their meteoric rise to fame; their lives, loves, music, guru, and philosophy; the big break-up, and what's happening now. It's the perfect way to recapture the whole wild, wonderful musical era while winging your way on your own magical mystery tour with

THE BEATLES TRIVIA QUIZ BOOK

Other SIGNET Books for the Trivia Fan

☐ **THE ELVIS PRESLEY TRIVIA QUIZ BOOK** by Helen Rosenbaum. (#W8178—$1.50)

☐ **THE FABULOUS FIFTIES QUIZ BOOK** by Bart Andrews with Brad Dunning. (#W8116—$1.50)

☐ **THE OFFICIAL TV TRIVIA QUIZ BOOK** by Bart Andrews. (#Y6363—$1.25)

☐ **THE OFFICIAL TV TRIVIA QUIZ BOOK #2** by Bart Andrews. (#W8410—$1.50)

☐ **FROM *THE BLOB* TO *STAR WARS*: The Science Fiction Movie Quiz Book** by Bart Andrews. (#W7948—$1.50)

☐ **THE TREKKIE QUIZ BOOK** by Bart Andrews. (#W8413—$1.50)

☐ **THE OFFICIAL MOVIE TRIVIA QUIZ BOOK #2** by Martin A. Gross. (#W7898—$1.50)

☐ **THE NOSTALGIA QUIZ BOOK** by Martin A. Gross. (#W7384—$1.50)

☐ **THE NOSTALGIA QUIZ BOOK #2** by Martin A. Gross. (#Y6554—$1.25)

☐ **THE NOSTALGIA QUIZ BOOK #3** by Martin A. Gross. (#W8412—$1.50)

☐ **THE SPORTS NOSTALGIA QUIZ BOOK** by Zander Hollander and David Schulz. (#Y6318—$1.25)

☐ **THE SPORTS NOSTALGIA QUIZ BOOK** by Zander Hollander and David Schulz. (#W7365—$1.50)

THE NEW AMERICAN LIBRARY, INC.
P.O. Box 999, Bergenfield, New Jersey 07621

Please send me the SIGNET BOOKS I have checked above. I am enclosing $_____ (please add 50¢ to this order to cover postage and handling). Send check or money order—no cash or C.O.D.'s. Prices and numbers are subject to change without notice.

Name_____

Address_____

City_____ State_____ Zip Code_____
Allow at least 4 weeks for delivery

The Beatles Trivia Quiz Book

by
Helen Rosenbaum

A SIGNET BOOK
NEW AMERICAN LIBRARY
TIMES MIRROR

NAL BOOKS ARE ALSO AVAILABLE AT DISCOUNTS IN BULK QUANTITY FOR INDUSTRIAL OR SALES-PROMOTIONAL USE. FOR DETAILS, WRITE TO PREMIUM MARKETING DIVISION, NEW AMERICAN LIBRARY, INC., 1301 AVENUE OF THE AMERICAS, NEW YORK, NEW YORK 10019.

COPYRIGHT © 1978 BY HELEN ROSENBAUM

All rights reserved

SIGNET TRADEMARK REG. U.S. PAT. OFF. AND FOREIGN COUNTRIES
REGISTERED TRADEMARK—MARCA REGISTRADA
HECHO EN CHICAGO, U.S.A.

SIGNET, SIGNET CLASSICS, MENTOR, PLUME AND MERIDIAN BOOKS
are published by The New American Library, Inc.,
1301 Avenue of the Americas, New York, New York 10019

FIRST PRINTING, AUGUST, 1978

1 2 3 4 5 6 7 8 9

PRINTED IN THE UNITED STATES OF AMERICA

*For Howard Colson
who discovered
my rock and roll soul
and gave me my
first byline, circa Fabian.*

The Mop Top Memorial Award to The Fab Four: Robert Earle Haynie, Arlene and Jerry Gross, and Margaret Richey for soothing my Beatle brain beyond the call of duty.

QUESTIONS

1. BIRTH OF THE BEATLES

1. Name the skiffle group John formed in his mid-teens, which he invited Paul to join.

2. Identify the school John attended at the time which influenced his choice of the group's name.

3. What was the name of the group George disbanded to join John and Paul in 1958?

4. John and the group were briefly known as Johnny and the ———.

5. While attending art school, John asked a classmate to learn bass guitar and join his group. Name this reluctant bassist.

6. The group soon began calling themselves The ——— Beatles.

7. The early foursome sometimes used these stage names:
   Johnny ———
   ——— Harrison
   Paul ———
   Stu— ———

8. Identify the drummer they hired for a tour of Scotland with Johnny Gentle.

9. Who was a temporary replacement for the group's first drummer? (Later he issued an album with the intriguing title ——— *of The Beatles*, destined to confuse record buyers.)

10. Name the Liverpool club this drummer's mother operated.

2. BEATLES: IN THE BEGINNING

1. Identify The Beatles first manager.

2. What was the name of the earliest in a series of Liverpool clubs their manager ran?

3. The Cavern was located on ——— Street.

4. Ringo was the drummer in what rock group before joining The Beatles?

5. Identify the club where the Beatles performed and met Ringo playing in the house band.

6. In what city was this club located?

7. When backing up Tony Sheridan, The Beatles were mainly credited as The ——— Brothers.

8. Who produced the early Tony Sheridan cuts with The Beatles?

9. John was influenced in his final choice of the name "Beatles" after Buddy Holly and the ———.

10. Name The Beatles first hit single, released in Britain in 1962.

3. BRIAN EPSTEIN

1. Name Brian's mother and brother.

2. Identify the school where Brian studied acting.

3. Brian set up a record department in his family's chain of ———— stores.

4. In what year was Brian first made aware of The Beatles, when record customers began requesting their early release? What was the title of this early Beatles record, on which they backed Tony Sheridan?

5. In what country was this attention-getting Beatles disc recorded?

6. Name the Liverpool club where Brian first saw The Beatles perform.

7. With Brian as their new manager, ——— Records was the first company to turn down The Beatles for a recording contract.

8. Brian finally secured a recording contract in England for The Beatles with ———, a division of EMI.

9. The Epstein entertainment empire was known as NEMS Enterprises. The initials NEMS stood for what earlier business of Brian's?

10. What was the date of Brian's death? How old was he at the time of his death?

4. THE BEATLE BLITZ: IN RECORD TIME

1. Name the label for which The Beatles made their early recordings with Tony Sheridan.

2. The bootleg Hamburg tapes surfaced on an album called *The ―――― Young Beatles*.

3. Identify the first American record company authorized to issue Beatles releases.

4. Along with The Beatles, who was featured on the album *Jolly, What!*?

5. A double album, billed on the cover as *The International Battle of the Century*, had The Beatles vs. which American group?

6. The album *Introducing The Beatles—England's No. 1 Vocal Group* was repackaged under what title?

7. What was the first Beatles single to hit the No. 1 position on the American charts? Give the year.

8. Identify the first Beatles album issued in America by Capitol.

9. Name The Beatles' record producer of eight years.

10. The Beatles' music publishing firm is called ―――― Songs.

5. BEATLEMANIA STRIKES AMERICA!

1. Who introduced The Beatles to America via a videotape played on his TV show in early January, 1964?

2. Give the date The Beatles first arrived in America. In what city did they land?

3. Identify the date of The Beatles' first appearance on *The Ed Sullivan Show*.

4. Name the concert promoter responsible for bringing The Beatles to the United States.

5. The Beatles performed their first live American concert at the ——— Coliseum. What was the date?

6. They made their second appearance on *The Ed Sullivan Show* from the ——— Hotel. In what city is this hotel located? Give the date of the group's second appearance.

7. The Beatles' second American tour began with a concert at the San Francisco ——— Palace. What was the date?

8. The following year The Beatles appeared at Shea Stadium. Behind which base was the stage located?

9. Their third and last major tour of the United States was kicked off at the ——— Amphitheatre. What was the date?

10. While in New York on their last American tour, The Beatles stayed at the ——— Hotel.

6. THE BEATLE BEAT

Match the Beatle album to the year of its original American release.

1. *Rock 'N' Roll Music*   a. 1964

2. *Sgt. Pepper's Lonely Hearts Club Band*   b. 1965

3. *Yellow Submarine*   c. 1966

4. *Help!*   d. 1967

5. *The Beatles 1962-66*   e. 1968

6. *Love Songs*   f. 1969

7. *Something New*   g. 1970

8. *The Beatles*   h. 1973

9. *Yesterday . . . And Today*   i 1976

10. *Hey Jude*   j. 1977

7. THE FAB FOUR ADD UP TO MORE

Fill in the blanks using Beatle arithmetic to complete the following song titles.

1. "Not a ——— Time"

2. "——— Days a Week"

3. "When I'm ——— -Four"

4. "——— and One Is Two"

5. "One After ———"

6. "Sweet Little ———"

7. "——— Cool Cats"

8. "——— Days"

9. "——— Legs"

10. "——— of Us"

8. PAUL: HE MUST HAVE BEEN A BEAUTIFUL BABY

1. What is the date of Paul's birth?

2. Paul plays ―― guitar.

3. Identify Paul's sun sign.

4. Give the full name of Paul's younger brother.

5. Identify his brother's group.

6. Paul adopted Linda's daughter ―― by her first marriage.

7. Give the first names of Paul and Linda's two other daughters.

8. The McCartneys' first son was born in 1977. Give the boy's first and middle names.

9. What is Paul's real first name?

10. Paul is actually his ―― name.

9. "I"

Keep your eye on these "I" songs by The Beatles, filling in the blanks to complete the titles.

1. "I Call Your ———"

2. "I ——— You"

3. "I Feel ———"

4. "I Saw Her ——— There"

5. "I Should Have ——— Better"

6. "I ———"

7. "I Want to ——— You"

8. "I ——— Around"

9. "I ——— Be Your Man"

10. "I ——— Mine"

10. BRIAN'S SUPERSTAR STABLE

In addition to The Beatles, were the following individual artists and groups also managed by Brian Epstein? Answer true or false after each name.

1. The Bee Gees

2. Cilla Black

3. Bob Dylan

4. The Cyrkle

5. Twiggy

6. The Rolling Stones

7. Cream

8. Billy J. Kramer and the Dakotas

9. Fabian

10. Gerry and the Pacemakers

11. ALL

Fill in the blanks, completing all these Beatles songs with the word "All" in the title, you all!

1. "All You Need Is ———"

2. "All I've Got to ———"

3. "Give It All ———"

4. "All ——— Now"

5. "——— Morning I Pushed an Empty Baby Carriage All Over the City"

6. "All By ———"

7. "All That I've ———"

8. "All My ———"

9. "Any ——— at All"

10. "——— on You All"

12. BEATLE BODIES: ANATOMY LESSON

Fill in the blanks, completing the body and soul of these song titles written and/or performed by The Beatles.

1. "Devil in Her ———"

2. "I Want to Hold Your ———"

3. "Piece of My ———"

4. "From Head to ———"

5. "Tip of My ———"

6. "——— of Love"

7. "——— of the Country"

8. "Long ——— Lady"

9. "Baby's ———"

10. "Greasy ———"

13. LOVE SONGS TO THE BEATLES

Match these loving Beatle thoughts in the song titles to the artists who recorded them.

1. "We Love The Beatles"
2. "I Want to Be a Beatle"
3. "A Beatle I Want to Be"
4. "Treat Him Tender, Maureen"
5. "We Love You, Beatles"
6. "Yes, You Can Hold My Hand"
7. "I'll Let You Hold My Hand"
8. "All I Want for Christmas Is a Beatle"
9. "Bring Back The Beatles"
10. "Little Beatle Boy"

a. Angie and the Chiclettes
b. The Angels
c. Dora Bryan
d. The Vernon Girls
e. The Bootles
f. The Carefrees
g. David Peel
h. Sonny Curtis
i. The Beatlettes
j. Gene Cornish and the Unbeetables

14. JOHNNY'S BIRTHDAY

1. What is the date of John's birth?

2. John was raised by his Aunt ——.

3. Identify John's sun sign.

4. Give the first three names of John's son by his previous marriage.

5. By what name is the boy known?

6. Give the first name of John's son by his current marriage.

7. John plays —— guitar.

8. He attended —— College of Art.

9. Give John's original middle name.

10. He changed his middle name legally in 1969. What is his new middle name?

15. BEATLE BIOGRAPHIES: JOHN AND PAUL (& SOME CLIPPED WINGS)

Match the titles of these bios about individual Beatles to their respective authors.

1. *Paul McCartney—In His Own Words*
2. *The Paul McCartney Story*
3. *The Facts About a Rock Group, Featuring Wings*
4. *Paul McCartney and Wings*
5. *Lennon Remembers*
6. *John Lennon—One Day at a Time*
7. *Paul McCartney & WINGS*
8. *Paul McCartney: A Biography in Words and Music*
9. *John Lennon: A Biography in Words and Music*
10. *The Lennon Factor*

a. Tony Jasper
b. Paul Young
c. Jeremy Pascall
d. David Gelly (Introduction by Paul McCartney)
e. Anthony Fawcett
f. Ken Barnes
g. George Tremlett
h. Jann Wenner
i. Paul Gambaccini
j. John Mendelsohn

16. MS., MISS, MRS. & MR.

Meet the following members of The Beatles' musical family by completing the titles of these songs.

1. "Lawdy Miss ———"

2. "Miss ———"

3. "Mrs. ———"
   "Mrs. ———"

4. "Please Mr. ———"

5. "Mr. ———"

6. "Being for the Benefit of Mr. ———"

7. "Dizzy Miss ———"

8. "Mr. ——— Man"

9. "Momma Miss ———"

10. "Move Over Ms. ———"

17. BEATLE FILM CALENDAR

Match the following movies, starring The Beatles or various members of the group, to the year of the film's release.

1. *The Concert for Bangla Desh*   a. 1964

2. *Sextette*   b. 1965

3. *Let It Be*   c. 1967

4. *That'll Be the Day*   d. 1968

5. *Help!*   e. 1970

6. *Yellow Submarine*   f. 1971

7. *Lisztomania*   g. 1972

8. *A Hard Day's Night*   h. 1973

9. *200 Motels*   i. 1975

10. *How I Won the War*   j. 1978

18. THE BEATLES COLORING BOOK

Fill in the blanks to provide local color to these songs written and/or performed by The Beatles.

1. "Little ―― Pills"
2. "Baby's in ――"
3. "―― Slumbers"
4. "―― Jay Way"
5. "Maxwell's ―― Hammer"
6. "For You ――"
7. "Old ―― Shoe"
8. "Blue, Turning ―― Over You"
9. "―― Submarine"
10. "Pure ――"

19. GEORGE: BORN AGAIN

1. What is the date of George's birth?

2. He was born in the —— section of Liverpool.

3. Identify George's sun sign.

4. George plays —— guitar.

5. How many children did George and his wife have in their eleven-year marriage?

6. Name the guitarist George's former wife has been linked with through the years.

7. How tall is George?

8. He attended Liverpool Institute High School with which other member of The Beatles?

9. After leaving school at 16, George worked briefly as a ——'s apprentice.

10. George is active in the National Society for —— Consciousness.

20. THE BEATLE NEEDLE: TELL ALL, SELL ALL, SYMPHONIC SWELL ALL

Match the titles of these assorted confessions and concertos recorded by various artists to the record companies which released them.

1. *The Baroque Beatles Book*—Joshua Rifkin
2. *Switched On Beatles*— New World Electric Chamber Ensemble
3. *Sgt. Pepper's Lonely Hearts Club Band On The Road*
4. *Hear The Beatles Tell All*
5. *All About the Beatles—Answered by Louise Harrison Caldwell*
6. *Beatles Blast in Shea Stadium*—described by Erupting Fans
7. *The American Beatles Tour*—Ed Rudy
8. *The Beatles Story*
9. *Pandemonium Shadow Show*—Harry Nilsson
10. *Off the Beatle Track*—George Martin

a. Radio Puslebeat News
b. Vee-Jay
c. United Artists
d. Island
e. Audio Journal
f. Capitol
g. RSO
h. RCA
i. Elektra
j. Recar

21. DAY & NIGHT

Complete the blanks, filling in these Beatle songs of day and night for listening pleasure that's so right.

1. "—— All Night"

2. "Day ——"

3. "A —— Day's Night"

4. "A Day in the ——"

5. "The Night ——"

6. "—— Day"

7. "—— Night"

8. "Good Day ——"

9. "—— the Night"

10. "Whatever —— You Through the Night"

22. BEATLES A.K.A.: ALSO KNOWN AS

Or, The Beatles by any other name. Match these alternate titles of albums, working titles of songs, other titles by which songs are known, and zany names individual members of The Beatles have used on record to their true identities.

1. "Scrambled Egg"
2. *The Beatles Again*
3. Apollo C. Vermouth
4. *The White Album*
5. *Unfinished Music No. 2*
6. "Auntie Gin's Theme"
7. Ohnothimagen
8. "Open Your Box"
9. "Unfinished Music No. 1"
10. "That's a Nice Hat"

a. "It's Only Love"
b. George Harrison
c. "Two Virgins"
d. *Hey Jude* album
e. *The Beatles*
f. "Hirake"
g. "I've Just Seen a Face"
h. *Life With the Lions*
i. Paul McCartney
j. "Yesterday"

23. A (RINGO) STARR IS BORN

1. What is the date of Ringo's birth?

2. Ringo was born in the —— section of Liverpool.

3. Identify Ringo's sun sign.

4. How tall is Ringo?

5. Give the first names of Ringo's two sons.

6. What is his daughter's first name?

7. What color are Ringo's eyes?

8. How did Ringo get his nickname?

9. His real first name is ——.

10. Ringo hitched on to a "Starr" from his actual last name of ——.

24. (IN PARENTHESES)

Match the following songs, written and/or performed by The Beatles and friends, to their subtitles, given in parentheses.

1. "I Want You"
2. "No Words"
3. "Picasso's Last Words"
4. "You Know My Name"
5. "Anna"
6. "John John"
7. "Ringo's Theme"
8. "Norwegian Wood"
9. "You and Me"
10. "Money"

a. (Go to Him)
b. (That's What I Want)
c. (This Boy)
d. (For My Love)
e. (This Bird Has Flown)
f. (She's So Heavy)
g. (Babe)
h. (Drink to Me)
i. (Let's Hope for Peace)
j. (Look Up the Number)

25. MARITAL BLISS-OUT: FRIENDS, LOVERS, EX-WIVES & SUPER-SPOUSES

Match each woman to the description which best fits her relationship to a particular Beatle.

1. May Pang
2. Maureen Cox
3. Jane Asher
4. Nancy Andrews
5. Cynthia Powell
6. Yoko Ono
7. Olivia Arias
8. Patti Boyd
9. Francie Schwartz
10. Linda Eastman

a. Married John
b. Wrote her memoirs after dating Paul
c. George's ex-wife
d. Married Paul
e. Linked with George
f. Ringo's ex-wife
g. John's ex-wife
h. Model who dated Ringo
i. Paul's former fiancee
j. Dated John

26. I'M

Fill in the blanks to complete the titles of these Beatle songs with "I'm" in record time.

1. "I'm Happy Just to ―― With You"

2. "I'm a ――"
   "I'm a ――"

3. "I'm the Urban ――"

4. "I'm Only ――"

5. "I'm So ――"

6. "I'm the ――"

7. "I'm ――"

8. "I'm Looking ―― You"

9. "I'm in ――"

10. "I'm Gonna Start Another ――"

27. WHO'S SINGING THOSE BEATLE SONGS?

Match the artists to their recordings of songs by The Beatles.

1. Peggy Lee
2. Peter and Gordon
3. Billy J. Kramer & the Dakotas
4. The Rolling Stones
5. Badfinger
6. Ron Wood
7. Rod Stewart
8. Johnny Winter
9. Harry Nilsson
10. The Silkie

a. "Mucho Mungo"
b. "Far East Man"
c. "Let's Love"
d. "Rock and Roll People"
e. "Bad to Me"
f. "You've Got to Hide Your Love Away"
g. "I Wanna Be Your Man"
h. "A World Without Love"
i. "Mine for Me"
j. "Come and Get It"

28. DON'T

Do *complete these Beatles "Don't" songs by filling in the blanks.*

1. "Don't —— Me"

2. "Don't Let Me ——"

3. "I Don't Want to —— You Again"

4. "I Don't Want to —— the Party"

5. "I Don't Want to Be a —— Mama"

6. "—— Don't"

7. "Don't —— Me By"

8. "Why Don't We Do It in the ——?"

9. "Don't Let Me —— Too Long"

10. "It Don't —— Easy"

29. LINDA EASTMAN

1. Name the former New York rock music emporium where Linda served as house photographer.

2. What is Linda's middle name?

3. Identify Linda's first husband.

4. What is her first husband's profession?

5. Name the magazine where Linda worked as a receptionist.

6. Give the title under which Linda's photography book was published in the United States.

7. Linda's father and brother serve as her husband Paul's ―――.

8. Name the first rock music group Linda photographed.

9. What is the name of the New York high school from which Linda graduated?

10. Linda's high school yearbook contained this capsule comment about her: "Yen for ―――."

30. SOUR NOTES: BEATLE PUT-ONS, PUT-DOWNS & PROTEST SONGS

Match each "witty" ditty about The Beatles, which somehow never quite made the national Top 40 charts, to the individual artist or group who recorded it.

1. "The Boy With the Beatle Hair"
2. "The Beatles Barber"
3. "My Boyfriend Got a Beatle Haircut"
4. "I Want to Hold Your Hair"
5. "Beatle Stomp"
6. "I'm Better Than The Beatles"
7. "Yeah, Yeah"
8. "I Hate The Beatles"
9. "Frankenstein Meets The Beatles"
10. "Let's Bug The Beatles"

a. The Bedbugs
b. The Exterminators
c. Jekyll and Hyde
d. Donna Lynn
e. The Swans
f. The Insects
g. The Bagels
h. Scott Douglas
i. Brad Berwick and the Bugs
j. Allan Sherman

31. PAUL'S "DEATH"

1. In what year did Paul supposedly die?

2. How did he "die"?

3. What eerie message could be heard by playing the words "number nine" counterclockwise on the record "Revolution 9"?

4. At the end of "Strawberry Fields Forever," John is heard to comment, "I ─── Paul."

5. Give the symbolic license plate of the Volkswagen on the *Abbey Road* album cover.

6. Name the winner of the Paul McCartney lookalike contest, to replace Paul after his "death."

7. What is George dressed as on the *Abbey Road* album cover?

8. How did some fans interpret the initials O.P.D. on Paul's armpatch, pictured inside the *Sgt. Pepper* album sleeve?

9. According to The Beatles' claim, what did the initials O.P.D. on the patch actually stand for?

10. What color carnation does Paul wear in the *Magical Mystery Tour* booklet? What color carnations do the other Beatles wear?

33

32. THE BIRDS AND THE BEATLES

Fill in the blanks by matching them to the list of girls' names, completing the correct title of each song.

1. "Sneaking —— Through the Alley"   a. Eleanor

2. "—— Parker"   b. Lucy

3. "What's the News ——?"   c. Anne

4. "—— Rigby"   d. Suzy

5. "My ——"   e. Fanny

6. "Walking in the Park With ——"   f. Ruby

7. "—— in the Sky With Diamonds"   g. Bonnie

8. "Short Fat ——"   h. Sally

9. "San Ferry ——"   i. Maryjane

10. "—— Baby"   j. Eloise

33. BEATLE MOVIE MUSIC

Match these songs to the Beatles movies in which they were performed, or to the British or American soundtrack albums to which they were added.

1. "March of the Meanies"
2. "Telegram Sam"
3. "Another Hard Day's Night"
4. "Trespassers Will Be Eaten"
5. "Penny Lane"
6. "I've Got a Feeling"
7. "If I Fell"
8. "Beware of Darkness"
9. "Jump into the Fire"
10. "Microbes"

a. *Let It Be*
b. *Wonderwall*
c. *Magical Mystery Tour*
d. *Born to Boogie*
e. *Son of Dracula*
f. *Live and Let Die*
g. *Yellow Submarine*
h. *Help!*
i. *The Concert for Bangla Desh*
j. *A Hard Day's Night*

34. MARRIAGE, McCARTNEY STYLE

1. In what year did Linda first meet Paul?

2. Name the London club where their initial meeting took place.

3. Give the date of Linda's marriage to Paul. Was Linda's daughter by her first marriage present at the ceremony?

4. In what country were the McCartneys married? Who performed the ceremony?

5. Where did the wedding ceremony take place? Which members of The Beatles attended?

6. Who served as Paul's best man?

7. Name the other witness and his relationship to The Beatles.

8. Identify the church where Paul and Linda went after the ceremony to have their marriage blessed.

9. Who conferred the blessing?

10. When was Paul and Linda's first child born?

35. BEATLES LOVE MATCH

Fill in the blanks by matching them to the list of words completing the titles of these love songs any of The Beatles wrote, produced, or recorded themselves or for/with others.

1. "—— Me Love"   a. Oh

2. "Can't —— Me Love"   b. Song

3. "Love You ——"   c. Strange

4. "Love Me ——"   d. Bye

5. "Love Is ——"   e. Buy

6. "Love Is the —— Thing"   f. P.S.

7. "Love in ——"   g. Give

8. "—— I Love You"   h. Do

9. "Bye —— Love"   i. Sweetest

10. "—— My Love"   j. To

36. BEATLE BABY TALK

Fill in the blanks, completing the grown-up titles of these baby songs The Beatles either wrote, recorded, or produced.

1. "Baby, You're a —— Man"
2. "—— Baby Cry"
3. "Baby, It's ——"
4. "—— Baby"
5. "Baby You're a ——"
6. "—— Get My Baby Back"
7. "Everybody's —— to Be My Baby"
8. "She's —— Baby"
9. "—— Baby" (You Know That I Love You)
10. "Take Out Some —— on Me, Baby"

37. AROUND THE WORLD WITH THE BEATLES

Grab your bags and match the location of your Beatle itinerary in song by filling in the blanks.

1. Kintyre
2. Memphis
3. U.S.S.R.
4. Egypt
5. Cambridge
6. Kansas
7. Attica
8. Araby
9. Venus
10. Liverpool

a. "―― City"
b. "―― and Mars"
c. "―― State"
d. "――, Tennessee"
e. "The Sheikh of ――"
f. "Spirits of Ancient ――"
g. "―― Lou"
h. "Back in the ――"
i. "Mull of ――"
j. "―― 1969"

38. YOKO IS NO JOKO

1. Name the title of Yoko's avant-garde book.

2. Identify the London art gallery where Yoko and John first met.

3. What was the year of their initial meeting?

4. Name the art gallery owner who indirectly introduced Yoko to John. What was the name of the gallery owner's wife, a pop singer once linked with Mick Jagger?

5. Upon meeting John, Yoko handed him a card bearing what one-word message?

6. What did John do in reply to Yoko's request on the card?

7. Yoko is —— years older than John.

8. Identify the country in which Yoko was born.

9. Name the college in the United States which Yoko attended.

10. Give the first name of Yoko's daughter by a former marriage.

39. GEORGE GOOFS OFF

Since George plays more than one instrument under more than one name on several records, we've zeroed in on the "real" George Harrison. You are asked to match George's song of fame to his crazy name on record, with the instrument he plays given as a clue in some instances.

1. "Badge"
2. "Edward"
3. "China Light"
4. "I Wrote a Simple Song"
5. "I'm Your Spiritual Breadman"
6. "If You've Got Love"
7. "You're Breakin' My Heart"
8. "Haven't Got Time"
9. "Elly-May"
10. "All Things Must Pass"

a. George H.
b. George Harrysong
c. P. Roducer (Moog synthesizer)
d. George O'Hara
e. Jai Raj Harisein (percussion)
f. George Harrison and Phil Spector as The George O'Hara-Smith Singers
g. L'Angelo Misterioso
h. Son of Harry
i. Hari Georgeson (acoustic guitar and mandolin)
j. George O'Hara Smith

40. MAKIN' MUSIC WITH THE BEATLES

Hit the right note by filling in the blanks, completing the song titles on this Beatles mysterious musical tour in which they wrote, performed, or produced the material along with some famous friends.

1. "While My —— Gently Weeps"

2. "Gotta —— Gotta Dance"

3. "Twist and ——"

4. "This ——" (Can't Keep From Crying)

5. "Bridge Over the River ——"

6. "—— Junk"

7. "Tell Your Mother She's Out of ——"

8. "—— of the Leaves"

9. "I Am Your ——"

10. "—— Music"

41. IN BED WITH JOHN AND YOKO

1. John occupied the bed next to Yoko's when she suffered a miscarriage at Queen —— Maternity Hospital.

2. John and Yoko were married at the Rock of ——.

3. Give their exact wedding date.

4. The Lennons billed their honeymoon as a "Bed-In For ——."

5. How many days did the event last?

6. Identify the hotel where this Bed-In took place.

7. What was their suite number?

8. Name the city where the second Bed-In took place. In what hotel was it held?

9. Give the date John and Yoko checked in for the ten-day happening.

10. Name the song recorded at the second Bed-In in John and Yoko's hotel room, with an all-star chorus of friends.

42. WANNA RECORD FOR RINGO OR GEORGE?

Here is a combined list of artists who have recorded for Ringo's label, Ring O' Records, and George's label, Dark Horse. Match the artist to the correct label.

1. Ravi Shankar & Friends
2. Jiva
3. Bobby Keys
4. Attitudes
5. Henry McCullough
6. Colonel (Doug Bogie)
7. Carl Groszmann
8. Stairsteps
9. David Hentschel
10. Splinter

A. Ring O' Records

B. Dark Horse

43. IN THE KEY OF B: THERE'S A SONG ABOUT EVERY BEATLE

Fill in the blanks, completing the titles of the songs by supplying the name of the Beatle worth singing about. The artists indicated recorded these songs. And now you can singo about Ringo. Can George Harrysong be far behind?

1. "You Can't Go Far Without A Guitar Unless You're Ringo ——" Neil Sheppard

2. "Crazy ——" Tom Paxton

3. "—— Beat" Ella Fitzgerald

4. "Ballad of ——" Mystery Tour

5. "John, Paul, —— and Ringo" The Bulldogs

6. "I Want to Kiss —— Goodbye" Penny Valentine

7. "Let —— and Yoko Stay in the U.S.A." The Justice Department

8. "St. ——" Terry Knight

9. "—— You Went Too Far This Time" Rainbo

10. "—— for President" Rolf Harris

44. BEATLE COUNTDOWN

Match the winning numbers, completing the titles of these Beatle songs.

1. Eighty
2. One
3. Six
4. Ten
5. 4th
6. Sixteen
7. 1970
8. Two
9. 1st
10. 15

a. "Loup" (—— Indian on the Moon)
b. "You're ——"
c. "—— Virgins"
d. "Only —— More Kiss"
e. "Early ——"
f. "$—— Draw"
g. "—— of July"
h. "—— Years After"
i. "Nineteen Hundred and —— Five"
j. "—— O'Clock"

46

45. FLYING HIGH WITH WINGS

1. What year was Wings formed?

2. Name the site of Wings' first live concert.

3. Give the exact date this concert took place.

4. English fans are members of the Wings —— Club.

5. Linda once talked about recording her song "Seaside Woman" under the name —— and the Red Stripes. Red Stripe is a Jamaican ——.

6. Much of the *Band on the Run* album was recorded in ——, Nigeria.

7. Identify the first song Linda recorded on which she sings lead vocal. In what album does this cut appear?

8. Give the years of Wings' world tour.

9. Name the Paul Simon song on the *Wings Over America* album.

10. What song did Paul write in honor of his Land Rover?

46. BEATLE MOVIE MATCHUP

Roll those credits by matching the following films in which the Beatles were involved—and the one Beatle-inspired film—to their respective studios.

1. *Help!*
2. *I Wanna Hold Your Hand*
3. *The Magic Christian*
4. *Raga*
5. *Candy*
6. *Son of Dracula*
7. *The Concert for Bangla Desh*
8. *The Family Way*
9. *Wonderwall*
10. *That'll Be the Day*

a. Commonwealth United
b. Cinemation Industries
c. Mayfair
d. Warner Brothers
e. Universal
f. Apple Films
g. Cinecenta
h. 20th Century-Fox
i. Cinerama Releasing Corporation
j. United Artists

47. FILLED WITH LOVE, LOVE, LOVE!

Fill in the blanks, completing the titles of these love songs The Beatles either wrote, produced, or recorded themselves or for/with others.

1. "Love ―――"

2. "――― Love"
   "――― Love"
   "――― Love"
   "――― Love"

3. "Love of the ―――"

4. "――― My Love"

5. "Make Love Not ―――"

6. "――― of Love"

7. "Drowning in the ――― of Love"

8. "You Always ――― the One You Love"

9. "――― I Love Her"

10. "Love ――― Ecstasy"

48. WINGS & THINGS

Try winging it with Wings by matching these past and present (mostly past) members of Wings to the brief descriptions (not to mention the brief associations).

1. Geoff Britton
2. Linda McCartney
3. Tony Dorsey
4. Thaddeus Richard
5. Steve Howard, Jr.
6. Joe English
7. Jimmy McCulloch
8. Henry McCullough
9. Denny Laine
10. Denny Seiwell

a. Former Moody Blue
b. Sax, flute
c. Guitarist—played with Thunderclap Newman
d. Selected by Paul over 50 other drummers at London audition
e. Toured with Joe Cocker and the Grease Band
f. Trumpet, flugelhorn
g. Wings' first ex-drummer
h. Trombone, brass arrangements
i. Keyboards
j. Seven years in the Jam Factory

49. FOR BEATLEMANIACS ONLY

1. Name the David Bowie hit John co-wrote. What are the titles of John's two books?

2. Identify the subsidiary label of Apple.

3. Give the name of the drummer who subbed for Ringo in 1964 on part of The Beatles' continental tour.

4. What do the initials of the MBE award stand for? On what basis was this honor conferred upon The Beatles in 1965?

5. In 1970, John's first wife married Roberto ———. Since divorcing Roberto, she married John ———.

6. Name the producer of the Beatles films *A Hard Day's Night* and *Help!*

7. *Let It Be* was directed by Michael Lindsay-Hogg. He is the son of what noted actress? The movie was produced by a former road manager of The Beatles; identify him.

8. Name the three Beatles movies in which Victor Spinetti was featured.

9. Keith Moon appeared with Ringo in which three films?

10. Who dubbed the speaking voices of John, Paul, George and Ringo as animated characters in *Yellow Submarine*?

50. BEATLE FILM CAPSULES

Match the titles of these Beatles films to the brief descriptions.

1. *How I Won the War*
2. *Born to Boogie*
3. *The Beatles at Shea Stadium*
4. *The Family Way*
5. *Yellow Submarine*
6. *A Hard Day's Night*
7. *Magical Mystery Tour*
8. *Blindman*
9. *Candy*
10. *Little Malcolm and His Struggle Against the Eunuchs*

a. Ringo as Candy
b. Cartoon based on The Beatles, outdazzling Disney.
c. George was executive producer
d. Ringo directed
e. Originally made for British TV, based on Beatles' own idea
f. John as Gripweed
g. Ringo as Emmanuel
h. Paul wrote the music for the movie
i. The Beatles' first film
j. Filmed on location in New York

51. RED, HOT & BLUES

Fill in the blanks, completing the titles of these Red, Hot & Blues (including two album titles) written, produced and/or performed by various members of The Beatles and friends.

1. "—— Blues"

2. "Birth —— Blues"

3. "Red —— in the Sunset"

4. "—— Homesick Blues"

5. "Red Lady ——"

6. "Sue Me, —— You Blues"

7. *Red —— Speedway*

8. "—— Blacksheep Blues"

9. "My —— Is Red Hot"

10. —— *of Blues*

52. LENNON ON THE LOOSE

Yes, a Beatle by any other name. Match John's records to the nutty names he used on the label credits.

1. "Beef Jerky"
2. "Bless You"
3. "Going Down on Love"
4. "Mind Games"
5. "Nobody Loves You When You're Down and Out"
6. "No. 9 Dream"
7. "Old Dirt Road"
8. "Scared"
9. "Steel and Glass"
10. "What You Got"

a. Dr. Winston O'Boogie and Los Paranois
b. Kaptain Kundalini
c. Mel Torment
d. Dr. Dream
e. Rev. Fred Ghurkin
f. Dwarf McDougal
g. Dr. Winston and Booker Table and the Maitre d's
h. Dr. Winston O'Raggaē
i. Dr. Winston O'Ghurkin
j. Rev. Thumbs Gherkin

53. SONGS ABOUT SONGS AND A BUNCH OF BEATLE BALLADS

Fill in the blanks, completing the titles of these sing songs and Beatle Ballads.

1. "―― Love Songs"

2. "Only a ―― Song"

3. "―― Song"
   "―― Song"
   "―― Song"
   "―― Song"

4. "The ―― Song"
   "The ―― Song"
   "The ―― Song"

5. "I Wrote a ―― Song"
   "―― Love Song"

6. "No ―― Song"

7. "Ballad of Sir ―― Crisp"

8. "The Ballad of John and ――"

9. "The Ballad of New York ――"

10. "The Ballad of Bob ――"

54. MOP TOP MAGIC

1. Name the flavor ice cream Baskin-Robbins featured in honor of The Beatles.

2. "I Love You Ringo" was recorded by Bonnie Jo Mason. She later became a superstar under what name?

3. "I Want To Be a Beatle" was recorded by Gene Cornish and the Unbeetables. Gene Cornish went on to become a member of The —— Rascals.

4. Identify both sides of the single recorded by John Lennon's father, Freddie.

5. A character on the TV show *F Troop* was named—— Starr.

6. What is the name of the London stage musical based on The Beatles?

7. Name the off-Broadway musical produced in 1974 by former Brian Epstein associate Robert Stigwood. (The show was based on a Beatles album.)

8. Give the name of the baby pictured peeking out of Papa Paul's jacket on the cover of the *McCartney* album.

9. Identify the song John wrote about one of Mia Farrow's sisters in India, when Mia and The Beatles were visiting their guru. What is the name of the song Paul wrote in honor of his English sheepdog?

10. Back Tracks: Name The Beatles' American licensing firm. This is really —— spelled backward. Ringo portrayed a pauper with what name on his April, 1978, American TV special? The character he played is really —— —— spelled backward.

55. BEATLE SCOOP: A GROUP TO KNOCK YOU FOR A LOOP

Match these songs written and/or produced by John, Paul, or George to the galaxy of groups recording them.

1. "Air Mail" (Tone Deaf Jam)
2. "Black Sails"
3. "God Save Us"
4. "Back Seat of My Car"
5. "Baddest of the Mean"
6. "Catcall"
7. "Lumberjack Song"
8. "I'm the Urban Spaceman"
9. "Yellow Submarine"
10. "Young Love"

a. The Mike Cotton Band and the London Welsh Choir
b. Elephant's Memory
c. The Bonzo Dog Band
d. The Masked Alberts Orchestra
e. John Foster & Sons Ltd. Black Dyke Mills Band
f. The New York Philharmonic
g. The Joe Jones Tone Deaf Music Co.
h. Fred Tomlinson Mounted Singers and Monty Python's Flying Circus
i. The Electric Oz Band
j. Chris Barber Band

56. THE BEATLE ZOO

Fill in the blanks identifying the fish and fowl, birds and beasties to complete the titles of these Beatles tunes.

1. "Rocky ―――"

2. "―――'s Garden"

3. "I Am the ―――"

4. "Little Lamb ―――"

5. "Everybody's Got Something to Hide Except My ―――"

6. "I Dig a ―――"

7. "Dark ―――"

8. "Single ―――"

9. "Hey, ―――"

10. "And Your ――― Can Sing"

57. THE RUTLES

1. Name the title of The Rutles American TV special.

2. The Rutles like to be known as the —— Four.

3. Identify the American TV program on which a film clip of an early Rutles sketch was first shown.

4. The Rutles got their mythical start at what club in Hamburg?

5. What is The Rutles' musical answer to "Help!"?

6. The Rutles played to capacity audiences at New York's —— Stadium.

7. Name the creator of The Rutles. Identify the character he plays as The Rutles bassist.

8. The founder of The Rutles is also a member of what satirical group?

9. Give the full names of the other three Rutles, along with their real identities.

10. The Rutles created a "legend that will last a ——."

58. APPLE CRISP

Match these groups to their single releases on the Beatles Apple label.

1. Brute Force
2. Hot Chocolate Band
3. Badfinger
4. David Peel and The Lower East Side
5. John Foster & Sons Brass Band
6. Lon and Derrek Van Eaton
7. Trash
8. Elephant's Memory
9. Iveys
10. Sundown Playboys

a. "Liberation Special"
b. "The Hippie from New York City"
c. "Road to Nowhere"
d. "Saturday Night Special"
e. "King of Fuh"
f. "And Her Daddy's a Millionaire"
g. "Baby Blue"
h. "Thingumybob"
i. "Give Peace a Chance"
j. "Warm Woman"

59. SHE

Here's a she-for-all Beatles free-for-all. Fill in the blanks, completing the titles of the following songs written, produced and/or performed by the Beatles.

1. "She Came in Through the —— Window"
2. "She's My ——"
3. "She —— You"
4. "She Said She ——"
5. "Can She Do It Like She ——"
6. "She —— Back"
7. "She's Leaving ——"
8. "Ain't She ——"
9. "She —— to Me"
10. "She's a ——"

60. BEATLEMANIA ON BROADWAY

1. Name the Paul McCartney lookalike in the show.

2. Paul's real-life double plays —— guitar.

3. The musical supervisor of *Beatlemania* is Sandy Yaguda. In the 1960's, he was a member of the pop group —— and the Americans.

4. In what year did *Beatlemania* open on Broadway?

5. *Beatlemania* is billed as "Not the Beatles. An incredible ——."

6. Disc jockey Murray Kaufman serves as a special consultant to the show. He was once known as "The —— Beatle."

7. By what name is this disc jockey known professionally?

8. Name the "Starr" of the show on drums.

9. Identify the rhythm guitarist in *Beatlemania*.

10. Leslie Fradkin plays lead guitar as a member of the group in the show. Identify the record on which he also served as lead singer, with session men including the real Paul McCartney, who provided the backing vocal and guitar work.

61. APPLE SAUCE

Match these big Apple artists, including The Beatles themselves to their singles for the label.

1. Jackie Lomax
2. James Taylor
3. The Beatles with Billy Preston
4. Doris Troy
5. Ronnie Spector
6. Chris Hodge
7. Ringo Starr
8. John Lennon
9. George Harrison
10. Paul McCartney

a. "World of Stone"
b. "Try Some, Buy Some"
c. "Working Class Hero"
d. "Taking It In"
e. "Oh, Woman, Oh Why"
f. "Get Back"
g. "The Eagle Laughs at You"
h. "Supersoul"
i. "Vaya Con Dios"
j. "Oo-Wee"

62. BEATLE HOT WAX WOMEN

Did The Beatles—as a group or individually—write and/or perform, record, or produce these songs themselves or for others about the following women? Answer true or false after each title. (Bootleg records count here.)

1. "Angela"
2. "Peggy Sue"
3. "Michelle"
4. "Rosetta"
5. "Barbara Ann"
6. "Sheila"
7. "Carol"
8. "Gloria"
9. "Lucille"
10. "Florence"

63. BEATLE OF THE MONTH CLUB BOOKS

Fill in the blanks, completing the titles of these books concerning the Beatles. Can the Nobel Prize for Literature be far behind?

1. ——— *to the Core* by Peter McCabe and Robert D. Schonfeld

2. *The Longest* ——— *Party* by Richard DiLello

3. *A Cellarful of* ——— by Brian Epstein

4. *The Man Who* ——— *The Beatles Away* by Allan Williams and William Marshall

5. ——— *Count* by Francie Schwartz

6. *Love* ——— *to The Beatles* selected by Bill Adler

7. *The Girl Who* ——— *With The Beatles & Other Stories* by Robert Hemenway

8. ———, *Hypnotism and The Beatles* by Rev. David Noebel

9. *The Music of the Beatles:* ——— *of the Gods* by Wilfred Mellers

10. *Murray the* ——— *Tells It Like It Is, Baby* by Murray Kaufman

64. BUSTING OUT WITH THE BEATLES

Fill in the blanks, completing the locations of these Beatle musical hideaways revealed in their titles.

1. "—— International Anthem"
2. "The —— Conspiracy"
3. "Mt. ——"
4. "—— State"
5. "God Bless ——"
6. "—— Desh"
7. "—— Studio"
8. "Goodnight ——"
9. "—— Light"
10. "Give —— Back to the Irish"

65. THE BIG BAKED ZAPPLE

Album Alley: Match these Apple and Zapple albums to their respective artists, including a bunch of Beatles and close relatives.

1. *In Concert 1972*
2. *1967-1970*
3. *The Pope Smokes Dope*
4. *Electronic Sound*
5. *Life With the Lions*
6. *Beaucoups of Blues*
7. *Space*
8. *Live Peace in Toronto 1969*
9. *Accept No Substitutes*
10. *Band on the Run*

a. George Harrison
b. Delaney & Bonnie
c. Ringo Starr
d. Paul McCartney & Wings
e. The Beatles
f. The Plastic Ono Band
g. Ravi Shankar & Ali Akbar Khan
h. John Lennon and Yoko Ono
i. David Peel
j. The Modern Jazz Quartet

66. THE NAME GAME—WOMEN

Fill in the blanks, naming the women The Beatles sing about in these titles.

1. "Dear ———"

2. "——— Wheels"

3. "Lovely ———"
   "The Lovely ———"

4. "Polythene ———"

5. "——— Mae"

6. "Sexy ———"

7. "——— G."

8. "Sweet ——— Brown"

9. "——— My Dear"

10. "Long Tall ———"

67. BEATLES A LA CARTE

Fill in the blanks, matching the food and drink to complete the titles of the songs The Beatles wrote and produced, as well as the one album included here.

1. Apple
2. Banana
3. Chicken
4. Fish
5. Wine
6. Meat
7. Pepperoni
8. Turkey
9. Water
10. Beef

a. "—— City"
b. "—— Jerky"
c. "——, Women and Loud Happy Songs"
d. "—— Scruffs"
e. "Thanks for the ——"
f. "Tandori ——"
g. "We're All ——"
h. "Shaved ——"
i. "—— Anna"
j. "Cold ——"

68. APPLE PAN DOWDY

Apple Scruffs or Scruffy Apple: Match The Beatles in their various guises and disguises to their single releases.

1. John Lennon with The Plastic Ono Band
2. Yoko Ono with The Plastic Ono Band
3. John and Yoko with The Plastic Ono Band
4. Paul and Linda McCartney
5. John and Yoko with Elephant's Memory
6. Yoko with Elephant's Memory
7. Wings
8. The Beatles with Billy Preston
9. The Beatles
10. Paul McCartney and Wings

a. "Don't Let Me Down"
b. "Let Me Roll It"
c. "C Moon"
d. "Imagine"
e. "The Mess"
f. "Sisters, O Sisters"
g. "The Ballad of John and Yoko"
h. "Instant Karma"
i. "Too Many People"
j. "Midsummer New York"

69. HEY BEATLES, WRITE ME A HIT SONG

From the pen of The Beatles to the mouths of .... Yes, fill in the blanks completing the names of the individual artists or groups who recorded these Beatles songs.

1. —— John: "Lucy in the Sky With Diamonds"

2. Sergio Mendes & —— '66: "The Fool on the Hill"

3. Joe ——: "With a Little Help From My Friends"

4. —— Hopkin: "Goodbye"

5. P.J. —— "That Means a Lot"

6. —— Black: "Step Inside Love"

7. Jackie ——: "Sourmilk Sea"

8. —— Murray: "You Won't See Me"

9. The ——: "Hello Little Girl"

10. Billy ——: "Sing One for the Lord"

70. BEATLE BOOKSHELF

Match these books to their respective authors, chronicling the Beatle years through triumphs and tears.

1. *The Beatles Forever*
2. *Growing Up With the Beatles*
3. *The Beatles*
4. *George Harrison— Yesterday & Today*
5. *As Time Goes By: Living in the Sixties*
6. *All Together Now— The Complete Beatles Discography 1961-1975*
7. *The Beatles—An Illustrated Record*
8. *The Beatles: An Authorized Biography*
9. *The True Story of The Beatles*
10. *The Beatles: The Real Story*

a. Julius Fast
b. Walter Castleman and Walter J. Podrazik
c. Hunter Davies
d. Anthony Scaduto
e. Roy Carr and Tony Tyler
f. Nicholas Schaffner
g. Derek Taylor
h. Billy Shepherd
i. Ross Michaels
j. Ron Schaumburg

71. WHAT DO YOU SERVE THE BEATLES FOR DINNER?

Here's some food (and drink) for thought from The Beatles menu of songs. Fill in the blanks to complete these main courses (and side orders) in musical trivia for a Beatle banquet.

1. "A Taste of ———"

2. "Savoy ———"

3. "——— for Two"

4. "Wild Honey ———"

5. "——— Moon Delight"

6. "Glass ———"

7. "Ten Years After on Strawberry ———"

8. "Mean Mr. ———"

9. "——— Train"

10. "——— Fields Forever"

72. "I" TRY

Match the letter representing the missing word to the song beginning with the title "I," written, produced or performed by your favorite Beatle guy.

1. "I Ain't ———"   a. Jeep
2. "I ——— Right Away"   b. Missing
3. "I ——— Love"   c. Found
4. "I Don't ——— Anymore"   d. Knew
5. "I Remember ———"   e. Pretend
6. "I ——— Inside Your Eyes"   f. Have
7. "I Don't Want You to ———" g. Superstitious
8. "I Am ——— You"   h. Care
9. "I Wouldn't ——— You Any Other Way" i. Fall
10. "I ——— Out"   j. Dig

73. THE BEATLE BUBBLE BURSTS

1. Give the year of Stuart Sutcliffe's death. How old was Stuart when he died?

2. John shocked the world in 1966 by declaring The Beatles are "more popular than —— now."

3. Tales of mismanagement flourished in regard to the running of Apple Corps, headquartered at 3 —— Row.

4. The Beatles' ill-fated Apple boutique was located on —— Street.

5. John returned his MBE in protest against British support of which two wars? And what Lennon album was slipping down the charts?

6. Name the manager/accountant John, George and Ringo selected over Paul's wishes in 1969, long after the death of Brian Epstein.

7. In a sarcastic comment on Paul's *Ram* sleeve, John is pictured posing with a —— on his *Imagine* album.

8. Identify the last film The Beatles made together.

9. In what year did The Beatles break up? Name the year the group's assets were ordered to be placed in receivership by the High Court.

10. Keeping it all in the family, Paul continues to be represented independently by the law firm of Eastman & ——.

74. BYE, BYE BEATLES: STEPPING OUT SOLO
(Assorted Wives and Non-Beatles Allowed)

Match these albums to their respective artists—no more singing the Beatle blues. In several cases, the former Beatle is credited with more than one album here.

1. *Sometime in New York City*
2. *Red Rose Speedway*
3. *Rock 'n' Roll*
4. *Ram*
5. *Blast From Your Past*
6. *All Things Must Pass*
7. *Wedding Album*
8. *Venus and Mars*
9. *Bad Boy*
10. *33⅓*

a. John Lennon
b. George Harrison
c. Ringo Starr
d. Wings
e. John Lennon and Yoko Ono
f. Paul and Linda McCartney
g. Paul McCartney and Wings

75. WINGS IN LONDON TOWN

1. Name the remaining member of Wings along with Paul and Linda McCartney pictured on the *London Town* album cover.

Fill in the blanks, completing the following titles of McCartney songs on the *London Town* album Wings sings.

2. "—— Children"
   "—— Your Children"

3. "Famous ——"

4. "—— Traveller"

5. "Morse —— and the Grey Goose"

6. "Don't Let It —— You Down"

7. "Name and ——"

8. "—— Link"

9. "With a Little ——"

10. "Cafe on the —— Bank"

BEATLE-INSPIRED FILMS
76. I WANNA HOLD YOUR HAND

1. What was the original title of this film before another type of production beat the screenwriters to it?

2. The story of *I wanna Hold Your Hand* takes place in what year?

3. Name the actress initially cast in one of the lead roles but who later turned it down.

4. Identify the superstar whose daughter took over the part.

5. What is the first name of this actor's daughter?

6. The Beatles stayed at The —— Hotel.

7. Give The Beatles' exact room number.

8. The Fonzie type character retitles one of the Beatles songs "I Want To Hold Your ——."

9. Who impersonates Ed Sullivan?

10. Name the director of *Jaws* and *Close Encounters of the Third Kind* who served as executive producer of this movie.

77. SERGEANT PEPPER'S LONELY HEARTS CLUB BAND

1. What is the family name of the Bee Gees?

2. Give the actual first names of the Bee Gee twins.

3. —— is the first name of the twins' older brother, also a member of the group.

4. Identify the Bee Gees' younger brother, who does not have a role in the movie.

5. Who served as producer of this film?

6. What is the name of this producer's recent smash movie, for which the Bee Gees wrote the musical score and performed much of it.

7. Name the rock star cast as Sgt. Pepper.

8. How many Lennon and McCartney songs are performed by Sgt. Pepper and the band?

9. What movie studio made the picture?

10. Name the actor in his 80's who adds his special brand of fun to *Sgt. Pepper*. In real life, he formed a comedy team with his wife, who is now deceased. Identify this comedienne, known for her scatterbrained antics.

THE FILMS OF THE BEATLES
78. A HARD DAY'S NIGHT

1. Name the road manager's assistant.

2. Identify the actress who portrays the girl on the train, who in real life later married one of The Beatles.

3. Which Beatle did she eventually marry and divorce?

4. What titled name does Grandfather use at the casino?

5. Grandfather is described as a very "―― old man."

6. This actor plays the grandfather of which Beatle?

7. Who does Grandfather bribe for use of the tuxedo?

8. What is George questioned on his preference for by an advertising man?

9. Identify the actress who portrays Millie.

10. Who plays the neurotic TV director?

79. HELP!

1. What was this movie supposed to have been titled originally?

2. The recording session is held on —— Plain.

3. Which Beatle wrote "I Need You"?

4. What animal does one of The Beatles encounter in a pub cellar?

5. This animal is calmed by whistling part of a symphony by what famed composer?

6. What is the priestess' name?

7. Name Professor Foot's assistant.

8. Clang's gang disguise themselves in the winter sports sequence as ——.

9. Name the Caribbean island to which The Beatles flee.

10. How is the sacrificial ring finally recovered from Ringo?

80. THE BEATLES AT SHEA STADIUM

1. Give the exact date of the concert.

2. In which of New York City's five boroughs is Shea Stadium located?

3. Press reports indicated that nearly 60,000 fans attended the concert. But what is the exact seating capacity of Shea Stadium?

4. Name the soul singer who appeared on the same bill as The Beatles.

5. —— Inc. was the rock group serving as one of the opening acts for The Beatles on the program.

6. What is the name of the orchestra performing at the concert?

7. Identify the dance group also booked for the concert.

8. Name the late Ed Sullivan's son-in-law who produced *The Beatles at Shea Stadium* for television.

9. In what year was the concert first televised in America?

10. Who sponsored this TV special?

81. MAGICAL MYSTERY TOUR

1. Identify the license plate of the Magical Mystery tour bus.

2. Who portrays the fool on the hill?

3. On what day of the week is the Magical Mystery tour scheduled?

4. The courier is known as —— Jimmy.

5. Name Ringo's aunt.

6. What is Ringo's aunt dreaming of?

7. Identify the hostess on the bus.

8. What is Mr. Bloodvessel's first name?

9. The Magical Mystery Tour bus was seen traveling on the —— Road.

10. What does John give the little girl on the bus?

82. YELLOW SUBMARINE

1. Which Beatles album provided the inspiration for this animated cartoon, plus several of the soundtrack songs?

2. Name the music-hating ogres.

3. What do these ogres first drain their victims of?

4. Identify the kingdom in which *Yellow Submarine* takes place.

5. Name the fruit used for attack by the ⸺ Bonkers.

6. Who sends the Yellow Submarine to rescue the conductor?

7. The conductor of the band is known as ⸺ Fred.

8. In what town does the Yellow Submarine find Ringo? What does Ringo later have in his pocket?

9. Name the Beatles song cut from the film version shown in the United States.

10. Identify the three other new Beatles songs which appeared in both the British and American original soundtrack of the movie.

33. LET IT BE

Do the Beatles perform the following songs in this documentary offering a rooftop view before they go their separate ways? Answer true or false after each title.

1. "Besame Mucho"

2. "A Day in the Life"

3. "Got To Get You Into My Life"

4. "Shake, Rattle and Roll"

5. "Oh! Darling"

6. "Dig It"

7. "Act Naturally"

8. "Across the Universe"

9. "Yesterday"

10. "The Long and Winding Road"

THE FILMS OF PAUL McCARTNEY
84. THE FAMILY WAY

1. On what play was this movie based?

2. Paul's musical score for the original soundtrack includes "Love in the Open ———."

3. Who produced and recorded the original soundtrack with his own orchestra?

4. Identify the character Hayley Mills portrays.

5. What is Hayley's married name in the film?

6. In real life, Hayley married the director of the movie. Name him.

7. Who plays Hayley's husband, Arthur, in the picture?

8. Arthur seeks guidance for his problem from a ——— counselor.

9. What relation to Hayley does her real father John Mills play in *The Family Way*?

10. Name the island where Hayley and her husband first plan to spend their honeymoon before the travel agent leaves them stranded.

85. LIVE AND LET DIE

1. Who plays James Bond?

2. What is the name of the Harlem nightclub?

3. Identify the Caribbean island where Bond continues his investigation.

4. Name the author of the James Bond novel on which this movie is based.

5. B. J. ——— sings the title song in the film.

6. Give the name of Paul McCartney's collaborator on the title tune.

7. Who did Paul record "Live and Let Die" with?

8. Doctor Kananga is portrayed by ———Kotto.

9. Lois Maxwell is cast in the role of Miss ———.

10. Clifton James plays ——— Pepper.

THE FILM OF JOHN LENNON
86. HOW I WON THE WAR

1. Name the character portrayed by John Lennon.

2. Jack Hedley is cast in the role of the —— Musketeer.

3. Identify the General played by Michael Hordern.

4. What does the General warn to beware of?

5. Troops are sent to North —— to set up an advance cricket pitch for VIPs.

6. Which war is Lt. Goodbody a veteran of?

7. Identify the actor cast as Lt. Goodbody.

8. Lt. Goodbody led the Third Troop of the —— Musketeers.

9. Who produced and directed this film?

10. Give the names of the two Beatles films he directed.

THE FILMS OF GEORGE HARRISON
87. WONDERWALL

1. What is the title of George Harrison's original soundtrack album from the film?

2. The movie had its world premier in 1968 at the —— Film Festival.

3. In what city were the Indian tracks recorded?

4. Who portrays Penny, the model with the swinging lifestyle?

5. Name the absentminded scientist played by Jack MacGowran.

Do the following songs appear in the film? Answer true or false after each title.

6. "On the Bed"

7. "Hari, Hari"

8. "Drilling a Home"

9. "Ski-ing and Gat Kirwani"

10. "Guru Lou"

88. THE CONCERT FOR BANGLA DESH

George Harrison organized this benefit with a little help from the following friends who performed at the concert. Did they all really appear? Answer true or false after each name.

1. Ringo Starr
2. Bob Dylan
3. Sonny and Cher
4. Ravi Shankar
5. The Rolling Stones
6. John Lennon
7. Leon Russell
8. Joe Cocker
9. Eric Clapton
10. Paul McCartney

BEATLES PHOTO QUIZ

1. Who plays this sly old man in *A Hard Day's Night*? On what grounds is he arrested while selling photos with fake autographs of The Beatles?

(ANSWERS TO PHOTO QUIZ APPEAR ON PAGE 154)

2. Loaded questions: Identify The Beatles album named after a gun. Which single has the word "gun" in the title?

3. Here's a rare photo of the preliminary *Beatlemania* album cover. Name the Broadway theater where *Beatlemania* was recorded live. (*Photo courtesy of Arista Records*)

4. *Help!*: The piano keys must be frozen as The Beatles vacation in the _____ Alps.

5. The Pepperland Express: Yes, one travels by Yellow Submarine. How many leagues beneath the sea is Pepperland located?

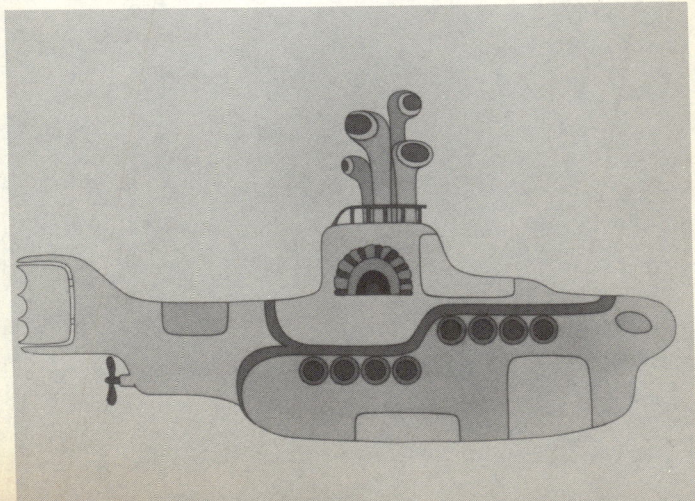

6. Name John Lennon's album with a similar title to The Beatles' *Rock 'N' Roll Music*. *(Photo courtesy of Capitol Records)*

7. What is the "doctor" attempting to remove from Ringo in this operation?

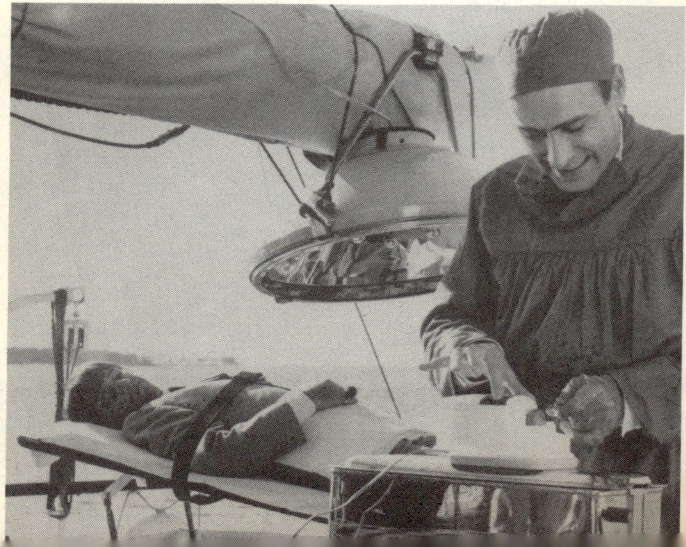

8. John and Paul briefly billed themselves as The _____ Twins.

9. Name the Goddess with eight more arms than Clang.

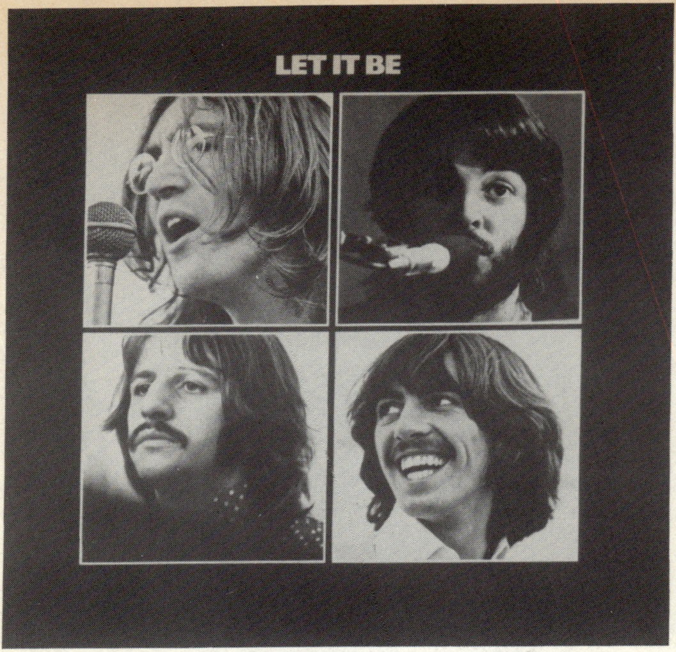

LET IT BE

10. Identify the three producers of the *Let It Be* album.

11. Instant Karma: What is the name of The Beatles' guru? Where is the location of his Indian retreat? (*Photo courtesy of Air India Library*)

12. Unscramble the word order, coming up with the title of the song John conducts in *Yellow Submarine*.

13. Open warfare: Give the site plus the exact date of The Beatles' last official concert. In what city was it held?

14. No ticket to ride: Name the actress sharing the motorcycle with Ringo in *Candy*.

15. Identify The Rutles' shifty manager/accountant mentioned in their TV special. (*Rutles photograph courtesy of The Rutles Corp.*)

89. LITTLE MALCOLM AND HIS STRUGGLE AGAINST THE EUNUCHS

1. This picture had its world premiere at the —— Film Festival in 1974.

2. In what capacity did George Harrison serve on the production end of the film?

3. Name the group performing the song "Not with You" on the original movie soundtrack.

4. Give the full name of the aspiring novelist played by David Warner.

5. What is Malcolm's last name?

6. Identify the first names of Malcolm's two friends.

7. Name the revolutionary group Malcolm sets up with his two friends.

8. What is the name of the artist whose painting the group plans to steal?

9. Identify the man this trio plans to kidnap.

10. Who plays Malcolm?

90. RAGA

1. Whose life does this documentary explore?

2. What instrument does the star of the picture play?

3. Name the state in which this serious musician is being exploited as a pop culture hero.

4. What is George Harrison's connection with this musician depicted throughout the film?

5. Identify the renowned violinist who plays a duet with the featured artist of *Raga*.

6. Name the two countries in which the picture was made.

7. A prayer meeting is conducted at the River ―――.

8. Name the Beatles firm which distributed the movie.

9. Name the young American musician who appears in the film.

10. This American was a member of what rock group with their own television show?

THE FILMS OF RINGO STARR
91. CANDY

1. Where does Ringo attack Candy?

2. Name Ringo's three sisters.

3. What has Candy ruined Ringo's chances of joining?

4. Identify the Swedish actress who plays Candy.

5. Who portrays the Welsh poet McPhisto?

6. Name the star of *The Godfather* who is cast in the role of Grindl.

7. What group sings the title song on the original soundtrack?

8. Ringo plays Emmanuel the ———.

9. Give the full name of the underground filmmaker.

10. Nurse Bullock is enacted by Anita Pallenberg. Offscreen, Anita shares her life with which member of The Rolling Stones?

92. THE MAGIC CHRISTIAN

1. Identify the character Ringo portrays.

2. Who plays Ringo's adoptive father?

3. The traffic warden —— his own parking ticket.

4. Name the famed English art gallery where the auction takes place.

5. The film includes what hit song written by Paul McCartney?

6. Ringo also appeared in *Candy*, based on a book co-authored by the novelist who wrote *The Magic Christian*. Identify this writer.

7. Who portrays the slave driver?

8. *The Magic Christian* is the name of a luxury ——.

9. Identify the man listening to the "lady" singer. (In real life he is a film director, although not involved on the production side of this movie.)

10. What is the name of the actor who plays Dracula?

93. 200 MOTELS

1. Name the two characters Ringo portrays.

2. Identify the town where the action takes place.

3. What is the name of the local restaurant?

4. Frank Zappa is the leader of a group known as The —— of Invention.

5. What does the group's manager appear as?

6. Name the orchestra this group performs with.

7. *200 Motels* was the first motion picture to be made in the ——-to-film process.

8. What is the name of the cartoon?

9. Name the song the hardhat cowboy sings.

10. Identify the folk singer who portrays Rance Muhammitz and the rock drummer who plays a nun.

94. BLINDMAN

1. Instead of a seeing eye dog, Blindman relies on a seeing eye ——.

2. How many mail-order brides is Blindman contracted to deliver?

3. Specifically, who are the brides intended for?

4. Name the character Ringo portrays, which is also the title of one of his other films.

5. What is the name of Ringo's sister?

6. Identify the blacksmith's daughter Ringo aggressively pursues.

7. In what country were the location scenes filmed?

8. Name the actor who plays Blindman.

9. Give the identity of the Mexican bandit cast as Ringo's brother.

10. How are the bandit's eyes put out?

95. BORN TO BOOGIE

1. On the technical end, Ringo served as producer and —— of this film.

2. In the opening credits, a still of rock and roll great Eddie —— is shown.

3. Name the lead singer of T. Rex.

4. How has this lead singer of T. Rex described the movie itself?

5. Identify the stadium where T. Rex performs live. What does the "T" in T. Rex stand for?

Are the following songs performed in the movie? Answer true or false after each title.

6. "Great Balls of Fire"

7. "Space Ball Pichett"

8. "Cosmic Dancer"

9. "At The Hop"

10. "Chariot Choogle"

96. THAT'LL BE THE DAY

1. Name the character Ringo portrays.

2. In what year does the movie take place?

3. Identify the leader of the rock and roll band.

4. Who is cast in the role of this band leader?

5. Name the rock star who plays Jim MacLaine.

6. What was Jim's first job after quitting school?

7. Give Terry's last name, which is the same as one of the original members of The Beatles who died of a brain tumor.

8. What professional drummer is cast in the role of drummer J. D. Clover?

9. Name the famed rock group this real-life drummer was actually a member of.

10. Jim buys a —— after walking out on his wife and child.

97. SON OF DRACULA

1. Name the American city in which this film had its world premiere.

2. In what year was this premiere held?

3. Name the character Ringo portrays.

4. Ringo is cast in the role of a ———.

5. What does Ringo shoot?

6. Identify the Christmas song from this movie.

7. Who plays the Son of Dracula?

8. What is the name of Count Dracula's son?

9. Name the producer of *Son of Dracula*, who also plays one of the leads.

10. This film was directed by what English master of horror pictures?

98. LISZTOMANIA

1. Name the director of this film, who also directed *Tommy*.

2. Identify the character Ringo portrays.

3. Who is cast in the role of Franz Liszt?

4. Offscreen, which rock group did this actor who stars as Liszt serve as lead singer?

5. Name the rock star who plays Thor/Siegfried.

6. Identify the two groups performing the musical score on the original movie soundtrack.

7. Who portrays Carolyn's servant?

8. Give the nationality of Franz Liszt.

9. What does Ringo forbid Princess Carolyn to do?

10. What is the spaceship shaped like?

99. SEXTETTE

1. Name the actress Mae West plays.

2. Identify the actor who portrays Mae's agent.

3. How many times has Mae been married?

4. Give the name of Mae's ex-husband, enacted by Ringo.

5. Identify the TV gossip commentator and talk show host who play themselves in the film.

6. By George: What are the last names of the two actors named George who appear in the movie?

7. What is the name of the actor who is cast as Mae's current husband?

8. One of the waiters is played by rock star ―― Cooper.

9. What country does Tony Curtis represent as a delegate to the peace conference?

10. Mae returned to the screen in 1970 after a 26-year absence to make a movie for 20th Century-Fox. What was the name of the picture?

ANSWERS

QUIZ 1

1. The Quarrymen
2. Quarry Bank
3. The Rebels
4. Moondogs
5. Stuart Sutcliffe
6. Silver
7. Silver; Carl; Ramon; de Stijl
8. Tommy Moore
9. Pete Best; *Best*
10. The Casbah

QUIZ 2

1. Allan Williams
2. The Jacaranda
3. Mathew
4. Rory Storme and the Hurricanes
5. The Star Club
6. Hamburg
7. Beat
8. Bert Kaempfert
9. Crickets
10. "Love Me Do"

QUIZ 3

1. Queenie and Clive
2. The Royal Academy of Dramatic Arts
3. Furniture
4. 1961; "My Bonnie"
5. Germany
6. The Cavern
7. Decca
8. Parlophone
9. North East Music Stores
10. August 27, 1967; 32

QUIZ 4

1. Polydor
2. *Savage*
3. Vee-Jay
4. Frank Ifield
5. The Four Seasons
6. *The Beatles—Songs, Pictures & Stories*
7. "I Want to Hold Your Hand"; 1974
8. *Meet The Beatles*
9. George Martin
10. Northern

QUIZ 5

1. Jack Paar
2. February 7, 1964; New York
3. February 9, 1964
4. Sid Bernstein
5. Washington; February 11, 1964
6. Deauville; Miami Beach; February 16, 1964
7. Cow; August 19, 1964
8. Second
9. Chicago; August 12, 1966
10. Warwick

QUIZ 6

1. i
2. d
3. f
4. b
5. h
6. j
7. a
8. e
9. c
10. g

QUIZ 7

1. Second
2. Eight
3. Sixty
4. One
5. 909
6. Sixteen
7. Three
8. Thirty
9. 3
10. Two

QUIZ 8

1. June 18, 1942
2. Bass
3. Gemini
4. Mike McGear
5. The Scaffold
6. Heather
7. Mary; Stella
8. James Louis
9. James
10. Middle

QUIZ 9

1. Name
2. Need
3. Fine
4. Standing
5. Known
6. Will
7. Tell
8. Lie
9. Wanna
10. Me

QUIZ 10

1. True
2. True
3. False
4. True
5. False
6. False
7. True
8. True
9. False
10. True

QUIZ 11

1. Love
2. Do
3. Up
4. Together
5. Greenfield
6. Myself
7. Got
8. Loving; Life
9. Time
10. Awaiting

QUIZ 12

1. Heart
2. Hand
3. Heart
4. Toe
5. Tongue
6. Hands
7. Heart
8. Haired
9. Heartbeat
10. Legs

QUIZ 13

1. d
2. j
3. h
4. a
5. f
6. i
7. e
8. c
9. g
10. b

QUIZ 14

1. October 9, 1940
2. Mimi
3. Libra
4. John Charles Julian
5. Julian
6. Sean
7. Rhythm
8. Liverpool
9. Winston
10. Ono

QUIZ 15

1. i
2. g
3. d
4. a
5. h
6. e
7. c
8. j
9. f
10. b

QUIZ 16

1. Clawdy
2. O'Dell
3. Vanderbilt; Lennon
4. Postman
5. Moonlight
6. Kite
7. Lizzy
8. Tambourine
9. America
10. L.

QUIZ 17

1. g
2. j
3. e
4. h
5. b
6. d
7. i
8. a
9. f
10. c

QUIZ 18

1. Yellow
2. Black
3. Golden
4. Blue
5. Silver
6. Blue
7. Brown
8. Grey
9. Yellow
10. Gold

QUIZ 19

1. February 25, 1942
2. Wavertree
3. Pisces
4. Lead
5. None
6. Eric Clapton
7. 5'11"
8. Paul McCartney
9. Electrician
10. Krishna

QUIZ 20

1. i
2. d
3. g
4. b
5. j
6. e
7. a
8. f
9. h
10. c

QUIZ 21

1. Tango
2. Tripper
3. Hard
4. Life
5. Before
6. Another
7. Every
8. Sunshine
9. When
10. Gets

QUIZ 22

1. j
2. d
3. i
4. e
5. h
6. g
7. b
8. f
9. c
10. a

QUIZ 23

1. July 7, 1940
2. Dingle
3. Cancer
4. 5'8"
5. Zak; Jason
6. Lee
7. Blue
8. He wore rings on several fingers of both hands
9. Richard
10. Starkey

QUIZ 24

1. f
2. d
3. h
4. j
5. a
6. i
7. c
8. e
9. g
10. b

QUIZ 25

1. j
2. f
3. i
4. h
5. g
6. a
7. e
8. c
9. b
10. d

QUIZ 26

1. Dance
2. Runaway; Loser
3. Spaceman
4. Sleeping
5. Tired
6. Greatest
7. Down
8. Through
9. Love
10. Riot

QUIZ 27

1. c
2. h
3. e
4. g
5. j
6. b
7. i
8. d
9. a
10. f

QUIZ 28

1. Bother
2. Down
3. See
4. Spoil
5. Soldier
6. Honey
7. Pass
8. Road
9. Wait
10. Come

QUIZ 29

1. Fillmore East
2. Louise
3. John See
4. Geologist
5. *Town & Country*
6. *Linda's Pictures*
7. Lawyers
8. The Rolling Stones
9. Scarsdale High School
10. Men

QUIZ 30

1. e
2. h
3. d
4. g
5. b
6. i
7. a
8. j
9. c
10. f

QUIZ 31

1. 1966
2. In a car accident
3. "Turn me on, dead man"
4. Buried
5. 28 IF
6. William Campbell
7. A gravedigger
8. Officially Pronounced Dead
9. Ottawa Police Department
10. Black; red

QUIZ 32

1. h
2. d
3. i
4. a
5. g
6. j
7. b
8. e
9. c
10. f

QUIZ 33

1. g
2. d
3. h
4. f
5. c
6. a
7. j
8. i
9. e
10. b

QUIZ 34

1. 1967
2. The Bag O' Nails
3. March 12, 1969; yes
4. England; Registrar E.R. Sanders
5. The Marylebone Register Office; none
6. His brother Mike
7. Mal Evans, The Beatles' road manager
8. St. John's Woods Church
9. Reverend Noel Perry-Gore
10. August 28, 1969

QUIZ 35

1. g
2. e
3. j
4. h
5. c
6. i
7. b
8. f
9. d
10. a

QUIZ 36

1. Rich
2. Cry
3. You
4. Sweet
5. Lover
6. Gonna
7. Trying
8. My
9. Ooh
10. Insurance

QUIZ 37

1. i
2. d
3. h
4. f
5. j
6. a
7. c
8. e
9. b
10. g

QUIZ 38

1. *Grapefruit*
2. The Indica Gallery
3. 1966
4. John Dunbar; Marianne Faithful
5. "Breathe"
6. Pant
7. Seven
8. Japan
9. Sarah Lawrence
10. Kyoko

QUIZ 39

1. g
2. d
3. i
4. a
5. j
6. h
7. b
8. e
9. c
10. f

QUIZ 40

1. Guitar
2. Sing
3. Shout
4. Guitar
5. Suite
6. Singalong
7. Tune
8. Lullaby
9. Singer
10. Sweet

QUIZ 41

1. Charlotte's
2. Gibraltar
3. March 20, 1969
4. Peace
5. Seven
6. The Amsterdam Hilton
7. 902
8. Montreal; the Queen Elizabeth
9. May 26, 1969
10. "Give Peace A Chance"

QUIZ 42

1. B
2. B
3. A
4. B
5. B
6. A
7. A
8. B
9. A
10. B

QUIZ 43

1. Starr
2. John
3. Ringo
4. Paul
5. George
6. Ringo
7. John
8. Paul
9. John
10. Ringo

QUIZ 44

1. i
2. d
3. j
4. h
5. g
6. b
7. e
8. c
9. a
10. f

QUIZ 45

1. 1971
2. Nottingham
3. February 9, 1972
4. Fun
5. Suzi; beer
6. Lagos
7. "Cook of the House"; *Wings At The Speed of Sound*
8. 1975-1976
9. "Richard Cory"
10. "Helen Wheels"

QUIZ 46

1. j
2. e
3. a
4. f
5. i
6. b
7. h
8. d
9. g
10. c

QUIZ 47

1. Scene
2. My; Let's; Young; Remember
3. Loved
4. Beware
5. War
6. Words
7. Sea
8. Hurt
9. And
10. Dance

QUIZ 48

1. d
2. i
3. h
4. b
5. f
6. j
7. c
8. e
9. a
10. g

QUIZ 49

1. "Fame." *In His Own Write* and *A Spaniard in the Works*
2. Zapple
3. Jimmy Nicol
4. Most Excellent Order of The British Empire; for "services to export"
5. Bassanini; Twist
6. Walter Shenson
7. Geraldine Fitzgerald; Neil Aspinal
8. *A Hard Day's Night; Help!; Magical Mystery Tour*
9. *200 Motels; That'll Be the Day; Sextette*
10. John—John Clive; Paul—Geoffrey Hughes; George—Peter Batten; Ringo—Paul Angelus

QUIZ 50

1. f
2. d
3. j
4. h
5. b
6. i
7. e
8. a
9. g
10. c

QUIZ 51

1. Yer
2. Control
3. Sails
4. Subterranean
5. Too
6. Sue
7. *Rose*
8. Cryin'
9. Girl
10. *Beaucoups*

QUIZ 52

1. g
2. e
3. i
4. a
5. f
6. d
7. j
8. c
9. h
10. b

QUIZ 53

1. Silly
2. Northern
3. Kite; Winter; Lumberjack; Star
4. Puppy; Honeymoon; Moonbeam
5. Simple; Simple
6. No
7. Frankie
8. Yoko
9. City
10. Dylan

QUIZ 54

1. Beatle Nut
2. Cher
3. Young
4. "That's My Life"; "The Next Time You Feel Important"
5. Wrongo
6. *John, Paul, George, Ringo . . . and Bert*
7. *Sgt. Pepper's Lonely Hearts Club Band On The Road*
8. Mary
9. "Dear Prudence"; "Martha, My Dear"
10. Seltaeb; Beatles; Ognir Rrats; Ringo Starr

QUIZ 55

1. g
2. d
3. i
4. f
5. b
6. j
7. h
8. c
9. e
10. a

QUIZ 56

1. Raccoon
2. Octopus
3. Walrus
4. Dragonfly
5. Monkey
6. Pony
7. Horse
8. Pigeon
9. Bulldog
10. Bird

QUIZ 57

1. *All You Need Is Cash*
2. Pre-fab
3. *Saturday Night Live*
4. Der Rat Keller
5. "OUCH!"
6. Ché
7. Eric Idle; Dirk McQuickly
8. Monty Python
9. Ron Nasty (Neil Innes); Stig O'Hara (Rikki Fataar); Barry Wom (John Halsey)
10. Lunchtime

QUIZ 58

1. e
2. i
3. g
4. b
5. h
6. j
7. c
8. a
9. f
10. d

QUIZ 59

1. Bathroom
2. Baby
3. Loves
4. Said
5. Dances
6. Hits
7. Home
8. Sweet
9. Belongs
10. Woman

QUIZ 60

1. Mitch Weissman
2. Bass
3. Jay
4. 1977
5. Simulation
6. Fifth
7. Murray the K
8. Justin McNeill
9. Joe Pecorino
10. "God Bless California"

QUIZ 61

1. g
2. d
3. f
4. i
5. b
6. h
7. j
8. c
9. a
10. e

QUIZ 62

1. True
2. True
3. True
4. True
5. False
6. True
7. True
8. False
9. True
10. False

QUIZ 63

1. *Apple*
2. *Cocktail*
3. *Noise*
4. *Gave*
5. *Body*
6. *Letters*
7. *Sang*
8. *Communism*
9. *Twilight*
10. *K*

QUIZ 64

1. Nutopian
2. Chicago
3. Elga
4. Attica
5. California
6. Bangla
7. Bombay
8. Vienna
9. China
10. Ireland

QUIZ 65

1. g
2. e
3. i
4. a
5. h
6. c
7. j
8. f
9. b
10. d

QUIZ 66

1. Prudence
2. Helen
3. Rita; Linda
4. Pam
5. Maggie
6. Sadie
7. Sally
8. Georgia
9. Martha
10. Sally

QUIZ 67

1. d
2. i
3. f
4. h
5. c
6. a
7. e
8. j
9. g
10. b

QUIZ 68

1. d
2. j
3. h
4. f
5. b
6. i
7. c
8. e
9. a
10. g

QUIZ 69

1. Elton
2. Brazil
3. Cocker
4. Mary
5. Proby
6. Cilla
7. Lomax
8. Anne
9. Fourmost
10. Preston

QUIZ 70

1. f
2. j
3. d
4. i
5. g
6. b
7. e
8. c
9. h
10. a

QUIZ 71

1. Honey
2. Truffle
3. Tea
4. Pie
5. Monkberry
6. Onion
7. Jam
8. Mustard
9. Gravy
10. Strawberry

QUIZ 72

1. g
2. d
3. j
4. h
5. a
6. i
7. e
8. b
9. f
10. c

QUIZ 73

1. April 10, 1962; 21
2. Jesus
3. Saville
4. Baker
5. Biafra and Vietnam; *Cold Turkey*
6. Allen Klein
7. Pig
8. *Let It Be*
9. 1970; 1971
10. Eastman

QUIZ 74

1. e
2. g
3. a
4. f
5. c
6. b
7. e
8. d
9. c
10. b

QUIZ 75

1. Denny Laine
2. Children; Deliver
3. Groupies
4. Backwards
5. Moose
6. Bring
7. Address
8. Cuff
9. Luck
10. Left

QUIZ 76

1. "Beatlemania"
2. 1964
3. Carrie Fisher
4. Paul Newman
5. Susan
6. Plaza
7. 1206
8. Gland
9. Will Jordan
10. Steven Spielberg

QUIZ 77

1. Gibb
2. Maurice and Robin
3. Barry
4. Andy
5. Robert Stigwood
6. *Saturday Night Fever*
7. Peter Frampton
8. 32
9. Universal
10. George Burns; Gracie Allen

QUIZ 78

1. Shake
2. Patti Boyd
3. George Harrison
4. Lord John McCartney
5. Clean
6. Paul McCartney
7. A butler
8. Shirts
9. Anna Quayle
10. Victor Spinetti

QUIZ 79

1. "Eight Arms to Hold You"
2. Salisbury
3. George Harrison
4. A tiger
5. Beethoven
6. Ahme
7. Algernon
8. Snowmen
9. The Bahamas
10. It drops off his finger

QUIZ 80

1. August 15, 1965
2. Queens
3. 55,300
4. Brenda Holloway
5. Sounds
6. King Curtis Orchestra
7. The Discotheque Dancers
8. Bob Precht
9. 1967
10. Clairol

QUIZ 81

1. URO 913 E
2. Paul McCartney
3. Sunday
4. Jolly
5. Jessica
6. Food
7. Wendy Winter
8. Buster
9. Dewsbury
10. A balloon

QUIZ 82

1. *Sgt. Pepper's Lonely Hearts Club Band*
2. The Blue Meanies
3. Color
4. Pepperland
5. Apple
6. The Lord Mayor
7. Old
8. Liverpool; a hole
9. "Hey Bulldog"
10. "Only a Northern Song"; "All Together Now"; "It's All Too Much"

QUIZ 83

1. True
2. False
3. False
4. True
5. True
6. True
7. False
8. True
9. False
10. True

QUIZ 84

1. *All in Good Time*
2. Air
3. George Martin
4. Jenny Piper
5. Fitton
6. Roy Boulting
7. Hywel Bennett
8. Marriage
9. Her father-in-law
10. Mallorca

QUIZ 85

1. Roger Moore
2. "Fillet of Soul"
3. San Monique
4. Ian Fleming
5. Arnau
6. His wife Linda
7. Wings
8. Yaphet
9. Moneypenny
10. Sheriff

QUIZ 86

1. Musketeer Gripweed
2. Melancholy
3. General Grapple
4. The "wily Pathan"
5. Africa
6. World War II
7. Michael Crawford
8. Fourth
9. Richard Lester
10. *A Hard Day's Night; Help!*

QUIZ 87

1. "Wonderwall Music"
2. Cannes
3. Bombay
4. Jane Birkin
5. Oscar Collins
6. True
7. False
8. True
9. True
10. False

QUIZ 88

1. True
2. True
3. False
4. True
5. False
6. False
7. True
8. False
9. True
10. False

QUIZ 89

1. Berlin
2. As executive producer
3. Harpoon
4. Dennis Charles Nipple
5. Scrawdyke
6. Wick and Irwin
7. The Party of Dynamic Erection
8. Stanley Spencer
9. Allard
10. John Hurt

QUIZ 90

1. Ravi Shankar
2. The sitar
3. California
4. Ravi Shankar taught George to play the sitar
5. Yehudi Menuhin
6. The United States and India
7. Ganges
8. Apple Films
9. Micky Dolenz
10. The Monkees

QUIZ 91

1. On a pool table
2. Lolita, Conchita, and Marquita
3. The priesthood
4. Ewa Aulin
5. Richard Burton
6. Marlon Brando
7. The Byrds
8. Gardener
9. Jonathan J. John
10. Keith Richard

QUIZ 92

1. Youngman Grand
2. Peter Sellers
3. Eats
4. Sotheby's
5. "Come and Get It"
6. Terry Southern
7. Raquel Welch
8. Liner
9. Roman Polanski
10. Christopher Lee

QUIZ 93

1. Larry the Dwarf and Frank Zappa
2. Centerville
3. The Redneck Eats
4. Mothers
5. An industrial vacuum cleaner
6. The Royal Philharmonic Orchestra
7. Videotape
8. "Dental Hygiene Dilemma"
9. "Lonesome Cowboy Burt"
10. Theodore Bikel; Keith Moon

QUIZ 94

1. Horse
2. Fifty
3. A group of Texas miners
4. Candy
5. Sweet Mama
6. Pilar
7. Spain
8. Tony Anthony
9. Domingo
10. With a lighted cigar

QUIZ 95

1. Director
2. Cochran
3. Marc Bolan
4. As "a piece of rock and roll and roll entertainment"
5. Wembley's Empire Pool; Tyrannosaurus
6. False
7. True
8. True
9. False
10. True

QUIZ 96

1. Mike
2. 1958
3. Stormy Tempest
4. Billy Fury
5. David Essex
6. Deck chair attendant
7. Sutcliffe
8. Keith Moon
9. The Who
10. Guitar